Exit Wounds

poems by

David Olsen

Finishing Line Press
Georgetown, Kentucky

Exit Wounds
poems of infidelity

With gratitude to those who sustain me, especially:
Paul Surman
Gwilym Scourfield
Hanne Busck-Nielsen
Dr. Anne Hammond
Dr. Barbara Schonborn
Dr. Patrick Henry
Professor Stephen Arkin
Dr. Jan Fortune
Leah Maines

ACKNOWLEDGMENTS

The following poems appeared in the journal or anthology cited:

Acumen: "Interval or Final Curtain"
The Interpreter's House: "It was only chemistry"
Orbis: "Language Lessons"
Poetry Salzburg Review: "Gelato"
Touch: The Journal of Healing: "Renovation Waltz"
Cinnamon Press "dark interiors" mini-competition #10 Runner-up: "Applied
Gemology" http://www.cinnamonpress.com/index.php/mini-competition-
winners-10

Publisher: Leah Maines

Editor: Christen Kincaid

Cover Art: David Olsen

Author Photo: David Olsen

Cover Design: Elizabeth Maines McCleavy

Printed in the USA on acid-free paper.
Order online: www.finishinglinepress.com
　　　　　also available on amazon.com

Author inquiries and mail orders:
Finishing Line Press
P. O. Box 1626
Georgetown, Kentucky 40324
U. S. A.

Table of Contents

"To say good-bye is to die a little."
~ Raymond Chandler
The Long Good-bye

Gelato

Embraced in the cotton wool
of Florentine summer warmth,
we lust for bracelets and rings
in Ponte Vecchio's emporia,
emerge into searing sun,
then retreat into the shade
of a strategic *gelateria*,
where smooth alpine slopes
glisten with gemstone colors.

I choose double chocolate,
but you ponder with slow
greed all flavors and hues,
tasting each with your eyes,
deciding at last on pale green.

We lean on the parapet above
a single scull's patient skim
along the green Arno's skin.
Beyond are terra cotta domes
atop tiers of honeyed stone.
You offer your cone for a lick.
Pistachio.

Renovation Waltz

The old terrace house had been neglected.
So much to mend now: shower, central heat,

forgiveness of paint. She was drawn by
the river's mauve and pewter dawns

and the wake-calligraphy of swans and geese,
grebes and gulls. She'd fled a violent

dissonance to start again with a new partner.
In a measured dance from room to room,

she's found confidence in restored grace
and the lingering *fermata* of a kiss.

Language Lessons
Cyprus

His exotic accent appeals
to your thirst for adventure,
your quest for something new.
In stolen moments between
conference sessions he begins
to teach you German, helps
you create a phrasebook.

Eager to impress with your sharp
mind and aptitude for expression,
you practice strange consonants
and learn the umlaut and how
to pronounce *ei* as *ī* and *ie* as *ē*.

As you acquire the spoken tongue,
he interprets your silent language;
in pursuit of certain success
he wants to know when to suggest
the action verb to transform
your faithful state of being.

The Dinner
Cyprus

It was meant to be routine—
two scholars with common interests
discussing their research.

You'd sat with him in conference
sessions and compared impressions
of speakers and their conclusions.

You flirted a bit, as one does,
when the attraction is mutual.
Surely there was no harm in that.

But he kept pouring wine,
recycling his best anecdotes,
scoring with tested repartee.

Freed of constraints of home
and work in this exotic place,
and unaware of his designs,

you were having innocent fun,
unmindful of his serious intent,
as you would learn after dinner.

The Spell

After the criminal assault
a warning lurked
somewhere in the primitive
self-preserving recesses of her brain:
the scent of a predator.

Despite the warning, she ignored

      his assertive self-confidence,

          recklessly bold approach,

      uncontrolled impulses,

          demand for gratification now,

      and indifference to her moral code.

She remained
under the psychopath's evil spell
no one but she herself could break,
unable to uncurl the breaking wave
of her tongue to say
No.

Trio

Unable to sleep, we try music.
Once a romantic dinner companion,
sprightly strings of Schubert's B-Flat trio
fail to soothe, and instead annoy.
Up for melatonin. Down to try again.
You try to read, can't concentrate.
I wait for exhaustion to overtake
the ache of mind. Today was the day
for you to say you've *met someone.*
Will this piece be forever ruined,
destined to become Our Song?

It was only chemistry

Hydrogen and helium were displaced
to the underside of a periodic table
turned upside down.

No man has ever treated me so well,
and I do love you, but now I know
I've never been in love with you.

I've never felt like this before.
He makes me feel I'm seventeen
again; it's a kind of madness.

My first reaction wasn't rapid
oxidation of trinitrotoluene,
but a slow burn of disbelief.

The Text

You returned home late,
exhausted from a weekend
of intense concentration:
writing on specified themes
and listening to readings
of dense textual weave.

While I hustled you to bed,
mindful of the working week
to come, I asked why you
hadn't rung me while away.
*I was tired. The sessions
were too intense.* Aware
you're usually in bed by 9,
I understood, but as the week
unfolded I still wondered:
Did you ring *him?*

I checked your phone to see
if you'd rung a number abroad.
By mistake I blundered into
your message log and found:
*Glad you made your train.
Thanks for a lovely weekend.*
In a fury I demanded the truth:
you'd been at a jazz club until 3.

Zombie

And again she comes home

exhausted
        haggard
                dissipated.

She slumps on the couch,
her jaw slack,
mind unable to focus.

Eyes have dark circles
        like bruises
as if she's been abused.

It's always like that
when she's been with him.

Is this the price of a thrill,
of escape from the mundane
while under OtherMan's spell?

Once, she loved a man
who granted rest,
healed her troubled soul—

four years
of patient care
negated, a waste.

chats with gertrude

when I enter the room
you hastily close
the live chat window

but not before I glimpse
in the header
the name gertrude

I wonder aloud
why a man would use
a female alias

does he disguise his gender
to fool the husbands
of his other women

oh no
you say
he explained all that

gertrude was his grandma
he honors her
by taking her name

Applied Gemology
The Four Cs

Carat:
The jewel is of good size,
but not ostentatious.

Cut:
The gem is well-proportioned
and of shapely cut,
with external sparkle
and abundant inner fire.

Color:
Color varies with ambient light,
often with a trace of blue.

Clarity:
Viewed with the naked eye,
this treasure possesses transparent
perfection, but close scrutiny
after long acquaintance reveals
a tiny heart-shaped inclusion
of unconverted graphitic carbon.

A Private Place

She'd allowed herself no tears at home.
After several days of wavering before
a weekend tryst, when her lover flew
to London to solidify his hold on her,
she's now resolute, intending to deprive
her once-trusting partner of any hope.

But in the isolation of her office,
she closes the door and sobs,
tries to regain control of tears
before she must attend a meeting
of staff, while wearing a mask
as if nothing's wrong. She's lost
her Best Friend, and can't explain
to anyone the real reason Why.

The Embrace

And so they cling together,
two welded links in a chain of events

locked in the urgent embrace
of their respective crises:

she, seeking a last adventure
before the stifling contentment of 50;

he, 16 years older, desperate
to prove he can still do it.

Pole Star

Two stars
    in close orbit

rotate round
    a common center,

oblivious
    to others

as if the universe
    is of no concern.

But long
    exposure reveals

their curving trace
    is one of many;

only the Pole Star defines
    the fixed center point.

Its constancy guides
    those who've gone astray

in moments
    of madness.

Ensemble

Saturday—once our day to lie abed
and talk until hunger drove us out.
As usual I offer to make breakfast,
but today, aware that in your house
the kitchen is mine, you ask to help.
Downstairs we move in smooth
harmony, as if performing a sonata
for viola and piano by Brahms.
We're as in tune as we ever were.

First drafts of poems from your time
in London await you, and we climb
the stairs to work on them together.
We find ways to compress a phrase
or consolidate lines; we agree
on just the right words, complete
one poem and move on to the next.
Satisfaction grows with each success,
as your original ideas acquire shape.
By mid-afternoon, four poems shine.
Oh, my love, we've had such fun!

Afterward, your mood goes dark.
Hard lines form near your mouth.
I wonder what I've done wrong.
Are you angry with me for some
inadvertent fault? Or do you grieve
for the last of our collaborations?

The Last Repast

Don't get me started.

I try to regain control
    of my contorted face
        and stave off tears.

Across the table
    she, too, is struggling
        to restore composure.

It's the first time
    I've seen her cry
        since her affair began.

She's been resolute,
    firm in her intent:
        there's no going back.

Tomorrow movers come
    to cart away
        my household goods.

She disrobes
    in the bathroom,
        all modesty for me,

chastely saving
    her alluring display
        for someone else.

For the last time
    I spoon her
        and try to sleep.

Disorder

The removal men have left,
their raucous voices gone; the scent
of their sweat and smoke dissipates.
At last the house is entirely hers.

Where paintings and prints once hung,
bare picture hooks stare from walls
where un-faded paint leaves void
rectangles of aching vacancy.

Cutlery drawers are in disarray.
Detritus of packing paper
and spent spools of parcel tape
litter the floors in every room.

Where his furniture has gone,
there are depressions in the carpets.
Replacements must be ordered,
tardy delivery men awaited.

A few indivisible items, bought
together in hope, remain;
others were carted away
to an address she'll never see.

What remains is the husk of a house
renovated in eight months of weary,
but joyful, weekends spent
building a home together.

The phone rings. The Other Man
calls from his home abroad:
Well done.
Now you are free.

The half-empty house fills
for an hour: promises are made;
obsession's quenched. She will await
the next call or text. Night falls.

Our homes live in us

When we met, you were homesick,
so I wrote a poem to remind you
of your family's summer cabin
by that lake in Maine. My gift
closed with *our homes live in us.*
You read it through tears,
wrote your own poem in reply.

You bought a run-down terrace house.
I helped you pack for the move,
entrusted with your long blue gown.
In eight months of weekends
we renovated your house, our home.
It was to be our happiest time:
building something lasting. Together.

On winter nights you came home—
glasses clouded with kitchen steam—
to a blinded welcoming hug,
a good dinner, Chopin, wine.
Your earned your welcome
from my friends. They, too,
created for you a sense of home.

How, then, could you make
homeless someone who'd made
a safe haven for you, aided time
in healing your broken soul—
who lifted you to your feet,
only to see you stride away
without a backward glance?

Fettuccine Alfredo

I grate a drift of *grana padano,*
dice an onion with sharp tears,
and melt butter in stainless steel
that reflects a fretted face.
In another pan I heat water
for pasta; grains of salt provoke
a fury of boiling. To the butter
and onion I add double cream
and stir in the cheese.

The sauce tastes as it always did
when folded into tender semolina,
but the missing ingredient is joy.
Once our favorite comfort food,
our Sunday sacrament is today
only starch and fat.

It is a truth

universally acknowledged
that when a woman dumps a man
she will try to retain him as a friend.

His constancy affirms her allure;
forgiveness confirms her worth.
A Good Woman has her reasons.

For his part, his hope's in vain.
She may appear to change
her mind, but only momentarily;

she was right the first time,
and he merely misunderstands.
When explaining to her mates,

she cites the mystery of chemistry.
It's all right. We're still friends.
Well, it isn't, and they're not.

Purgatory

We arrive separately
        to a meeting we always
                attended as a couple.

You sit next to me;
        we fumble a brief squeeze
                of hands under the table.

Others pretend disinterest,
        try to behave as if
                nothing has changed.

The urge to stroke your back,
        to rest my hand on your thigh,
                as before, is irresistible.

You turn to me,
        and fix an intense gaze
                on my eyes, and smile.

This is no passing glance.
        Your eyes condemn me
                to a lingering limbo,

a purgatory of ambiguity.

Interval or Final Curtain

Was that the last act,
or the end of the first?

The plot seems unresolved—
too many loose ends,
too many possibilities
for corrosive unfinished business.

People in black shift a bed,
move hands on the clock,
flip calendar pages,
place a wine bottle just so.

The players
(a goddess; a comic sidekick;
and a leading man,
less than gentleman,
more than shadow)
fidget in the wings,
uncertain whether to wait
for the safety curtain to rise,
or take off makeup
and put on winter coats.

Someone
should tell the players
if there's more to come.

Embers

Embers glow
with faint intent.

Shall they be stirred
to renewed warmth,

or shall they fade
to cold indifference?

Might our tragedy—
worthy of Puccini—

be resolved by waking
from a nightmare of deceit?

And would the will exist
to heal our wounds?

Performance Space

The safety curtain ascends.
Dim house lights
fail to illuminate
the bare inanimate stage.

Actors fidget in the green room,
rehearsing approximate lines
that may not survive
the absent director's cuts.

In the semi-dark
we grope for a pair
of seats halfway back
in the empty stalls.

While deprived of touch,
we keep monastic silence
as the weight of expectation
bears us down.

Something will happen,
but no one knows exactly what.
The safety curtain unrolls
to obscure the scene.

House lights come up.
There is no applause.
We depart:
north and south.

Before Me a Desert

With your usual grace
you tell me
Move on, as I've done.

Easy for you.
You're the exemplar
of how to move on.

That hot August night
you moved on with obscene ease,
bedazzled by prestidigitation:

fleeting touch of lips,
glancing brush of breast,
calculated testing,

before his bold decisive grope,
leading you to move on
to desecration of your temple.

Devoted to your care,
I had held nothing back,
never intending to move on.

Now you tell me
Take care of yourself.
Move on.

Before me a desert.
I have neither map
nor reliable compass,

and no clear destination
beyond a bare horizon.

An Honorable Retreat

You're perfect. At 48
your teeth haven't felt a drill;
a starlet would covet your figure;
you're so smart you seldom err,
rarely admit a mistake,
and never apologize.

You've invested so much
in a Grand Passion for the Ages
(which, if viewed from
the objective end of a telescope,
appears an overdone midlife crisis),
and transformed a holiday

indiscretion into a blunder:
disruption of our home;
damage to your reputation;
your emotional stake at risk
if he breaks your heart.
You can't withdraw with grace.

My constancy's of no avail.
Patience frays for want of hope.
So I'm left to contemplate
honorable retreat,
a belated letting go,
an overdue goodbye.

Enter Hero

You told parents, siblings, colleagues
only that you ended our partnership,
while remaining silent about your affair.
They were left to wonder: *What did
your former partner do to provoke
the breakdown of such a loving pair?*

You assured me: *You're a good man,
an innocent man, but life isn't fair,*
blaming "life" instead of your willful act,
while you appear to be the victim
of an undisclosed crime of mine.

You concealed your lover long enough
to ensure that his emergence as a hero
would seem unrelated to our parting.
You preserve your pristine reputation
at the expense of mine—while your
future life is cursed by lies and shame.

Peanut Butter Toast

If we reminisced or philosophized
in bed too late on Saturday mornings,

you wouldn't want to wait for porridge
with peanut butter and overripe banana.

You'd ask instead for peanut butter toast,
once proof against mornings in Maine.

I made yours with a butter underlay,
and trimmed the upper crust,

served it with Madagascan vanilla tea
we reserved for our weekend treat.

How long will I think of you
and Saturday mornings in bed

whenever I make peanut butter toast
just for myself and no one else?

Boutique

Neither shapely figure nor skin—
perfect, smooth, and pale—
arrests my eye.

It's the gown of elegant cut
in a subtle swirl of jewel hues:
violet, indigo, cerise.

Your colours—
those *you* possess
as if created just for you.

Oh, how you would look
in that fetching dress
with your long slim line

this mannequin
is meant to represent,
while failing the ideal.

Even on the Main Street
of a city you've left,
I still window-shop,

browsing here and there,
seeing you everywhere.

The Farther Night

In daylight I see no more
than ninety-three million miles—
eight light-minutes.

But if, in my solitude,
I wander into a clear night,
I see beyond the retired sun:

Saturn as an evening star;
Betelgeuse and Sirius;
the spangled Milky Way;

the chalky smudge
of a Magellanic Cloud;
the faint glow of galaxies

and nebulae—so far away
that their current events
occurred millions of years ago.

Just as I see farther at night
than in the day, in the dark
tones of a solo tenor sax

your face is there,
a constant constellation
in the velvet night.

Unfolding Origami (80pp, 2015) won the Cinnamon Press Poetry Collection Award, and *Past Imperfect*, his second full-length poetry collection, is forthcoming from Cinnamon Press. *Exit Wounds* is David's fourth poetry chapbook. Previous chapbooks include *Sailing to Atlantis* (Finishing Line Press, 2013), *New World Elegies* (Finishing Line Press, 2011), and *Greatest Hits* (Pudding Publications, 2001).

Since 2012 he has placed work with *Blueline, Lunch Ticket, Vermont Literary Review, The Aurorean, Pinyon, Pilgrimage, Pedestal, Bloodroot Literary Magazine, San Pedro River Review, Turtle Island Quarterly, California State Poetry Society Poetry Letter, Scintilla, Strong Voices, Touch: The Journal of Healing, Poetry and Business, Cyclamens and Swords, Ash & Bones, Devilfish Review, Wordgathering, Pyrokinection,* and anthologies from Main Street Rag (2), Concrete Wolf, Mutabilis, TulipTree, WaterWood, Blue Lyra, San Francisco Peace and Hope (2), and Kind of a Hurricane Press (3) (US); *Acumen, Envoi, Poetry News, South, The Interpreter's House, Frogmore Papers, Orbis, Prole, Proletarian Poetry, Sentinel Literary Quarterly, The Journal, Lunar Poetry, London Journal of Fiction, SAW Poetry, The Dawntreader, Gold Dust, The Stare's Nest, Morphrog,* and anthologies from Cinnamon Press (5), Templar Poetry (2), Belgrave Press, University of London's Human Rights Consortium, Albion Beatnik (2), Theatre Cloud (2), and Babel (UK); *Poetry Salzburg Review* (Austria); *The French Literary Review* (France); ROPES (Ireland); *The Deronda Review* (Israel/US); and an academic anthology from Sense (Netherlands).

A poet and playwright with a BA in chemistry from University of California-Berkeley and an MA in creative writing from San Francisco State University, David was formerly an energy economist, management consultant, and performing arts critic. He has lived in Oxford since 2002.